INTRODUCING THE OLD TESTAMENT AND HEBREW POETRY

UNLOCKING THE BIBLE VIDEO SERIES

DAVID PAWSON

ANCHOR RECORDINGS

Copyright © 2019 David Pawson

The right of David Pawson to be identified as author of this Work has been asserted by him in accordance with the Copyright, Designs and Patents Act 1988.

First published in Great Britain in 2019 by
Anchor Recordings Ltd
DPTT, Synegis House, 21 Crockhamwell Road,
Woodley, Reading RG5 3LE

No part of this publication may be reproduced or transmitted in any form or by any means, electronic or mechanical, including photocopy, recording or any information storage and retrieval system, without prior permission in writing from the publisher.

**For more of David Pawson's teaching,
including DVDs and CDs, go to**
www.davidpawson.com

FOR FREE DOWNLOADS
www.davidpawson.org

For further information, email
info@davidpawsonministry.org

ISBN 978-1-911173-90-8

Printed by Ingram Spark

This booklet is based on a talk. Originating as it does from the spoken word, its style will be found by many readers to be somewhat different from my usual written style. It is hoped that this will not detract from the substance of the biblical teaching found here.

As always, I ask the reader to compare everything I say or write with what is written in the Bible and, if at any point a conflict is found, always to rely upon the clear teaching of scripture.

David Pawson

Contents

Introducing the Old Testament 7

Hebrew Poetry 27

INTRODUCING THE OLD TESTAMENT

Instead of taking a book of the Bible here, I want to give you an overview of the *whole* Old Testament. Here we have a collection of books covering about a thousand years, written by many different authors and containing many different types of books. There are history books, law books, song books. How do they all relate together, all 39 of them? I think it is so important to have an overall picture of how these books fit together. God has not given us a topical Bible. Wouldn't it be nice if he had? You know, if the book of Genesis was all about God, and the book of Exodus all about Jesus, and the book of Leviticus all about the Holy Spirit, and if he had put all the text together under one topic it would save us buying concordances and looking things up from all over. He deliberately did not give us a Bible like that. He didn't want us to have a Bible like that and so the teaching on any one topic is scattered over the whole Bible. And he didn't want to give us a box full of texts, though since chapter and verse numbers have been added to the Bible that is how we treat it, and we pick a text out from here and a text out from there, and just ignore the context so often.

Well, God has given us actually a *library* of books. The word 'Bible' is a plural word; it comes from the Latin *biblia* and it means 'books', not 'book', so the Bible is not a book; it is a library of books, and each book is a separate entity.

God wants you to learn his word book by book because that is how he chose to give it to us. If he just wanted to give us a lot of texts, he would have done that; if he wanted to give us a lot of topics, he would have done that, but what he did do was give us these books and every text (as we call each verse) is in a context of that book, and that book is in a context of history. God gave us his Word in time and space and it is very important to get both dimensions, so that we understand at what time he said this, and in what place he said this, and the time and place give it its meaning because his word was given in life situations. He was always saying something to a particular situation in time and space, and those are the two contexts we need. So I thought in this section I would give you something of that context.

Let us begin with space, and to do that of course we need maps. There is a geography of the Bible as well as a history of the Bible that we need to hold in our minds when we are reading it. And there are really only two maps that we need: a map of the whole Middle East and a map of the Promised Land in the Middle East, and we need to hold these if we can as a picture in our minds. Now the familiar name that is given to the overall map of the Middle East is The Fertile Crescent and that is a phrase you will read in many books on Bible background. I have drawn the crescent, a sort of new moon shape, on this map and what it does is it links two very large rivers at each end – the River Nile and the two rivers Tigris and Euphrates, and those two major river basins produce fertility. So these are very fertile valleys, the Nile Delta and the Nile Valley and then the Tigris and the Euphrates – what used to be called Mesopotamia, which means the middle of the rivers: 'Meso' – middle, and 'potamia' – rivers, so between the two rivers – a very fertile plain, very flat. These two fertile areas were the centres of power in the ancient world; these were the east and west world powers. So the

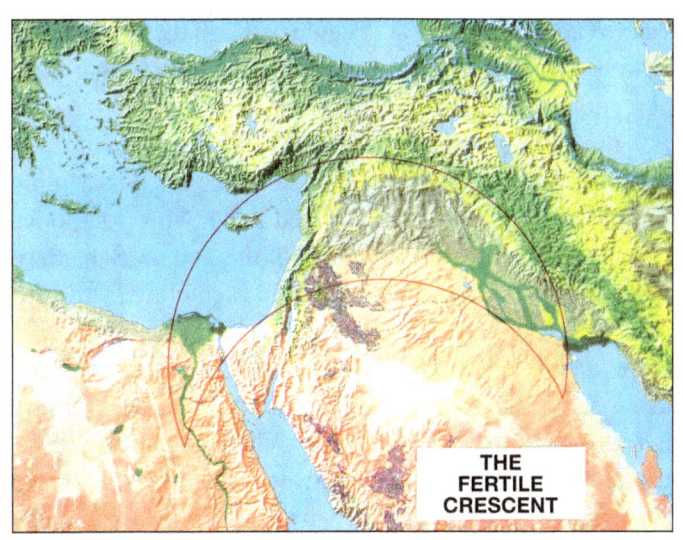

THE FERTILE CRESCENT

THE PROMISED LAND

whole Old Testament is a struggle between these two world powers – between Egypt and the different empires that arose here, notably Assyria and Babylon. That is where Iraq and Iran are now, and they are divided by a river.

So we have two world powers in the ancient Middle East and in between, the Promised Land. Now you notice that the Arabian Desert covers all of this and the Sahara, so when these two big powers attacked each other or tried to overcome each other they had to travel through this narrow bit of land. I don't know if you can see a rather darker patch that is actually black basalt rock which is very sharp and very hard – even camels can't cross it. Which means that all the traffic was directed down the narrow coastal strip. If you did not want to cross the desert (which most didn't) but if you wanted to keep feeding your troops, you had to go through the Fertile Crescent – you had to go round that crescent to the other end to attack your enemy. Which means that this was the crossroads of the world actually. Somebody has said about Israel: if you will live in the middle of a crossroads you are bound to get run over – which is exactly what happened. They were constantly being run over. In Jesus' day they were run over by the Romans but before that they had been run over by the Greeks and the Syrians and the Egyptians, and so it goes on. So here we have two world powers at either end of this crescent with a narrow corridor down the coast in between. God gave them a land at the crossroads of the world. Actually, the road from Europe to Arabia comes down through that corridor and the road from Africa to Asia goes through that corridor. On this map the road from Europe comes down the coast, it crosses the Plain of Esdraelon, goes down into the Jordan Valley and up on to the other side and down to Arabia. The road from Africa comes up the coastal plain and it crosses over the same Vale of Esdraelon or the Valley of Jezreel and goes up through Capernaum and up through Damascus and on to India and China.

The actual crossroads of the world is precisely at a little hill called Megiddo, and the Hill of Megiddo in Hebrew is Hamageddon; and that is why most of the big battles in history took place there at the crossroads of the world. Overlooking that crossroads is a little village called Nazareth, and a boy of Nazareth could watch the world go by. Literally he could lie on the hill as a boy, could Jesus, and it was like being in an airport lounge where you see all the nationalities coming and going. That is why they call the northern part 'Galilee of the Nations' because it was an international crossroads. Whereas further south, up in the hills, it was very isolated and very Jewish, and Jerusalem is right up in 'them there hills'. So you had two parts of the Promised Land: the international part where all the nations came and went, and the very Jewish isolated part up in the hills with Jerusalem. So you can see the importance of this land. God was going to plant his people at the crossroads of the world where everybody could see them, where they could be a model of the kingdom of heaven on earth. So the whole world could see what blessing comes to people living under God's rule, but they would also see what curse comes of disobeying God's rule.

So you can see why God chose this land. Now it's a very fertile strip. There is that black basalt. If you have ever been to Capernaum you have seen the black basalt rock. They used it to build the houses of Capernaum – terribly hard, sharp stuff. So it was impassable, so there was this barrier of sand and basalt rock on the east and the barrier of the sea on the west. All the traffic went down the coast and through the little break in the hills which we call the Vale of Esdraelon or Hamageddon. Then we have a huge crack right down the Earth's surface, right through to Africa, and here is its deepest point. The white bit is below sea level, and the Dead Sea is way below. You have the Jordan coming into this valley and going nowhere, just evaporating from the intense heat.

So in this little area the size of Wales you have the entire world in miniature. You have got every kind of climate and every kind of scenery. You will find somewhere in Israel a place like home. In fact the place most like England is just south of Tel Aviv. But they call Carmel 'Little Switzerland' and you can always go skiing at any time of year on the snow-capped Mount Hermon, yet ten minutes later you can be down among palm trees. All the fauna and flora of Europe is to be found here, all the fauna and flora of Africa is to be found here, all the fauna and flora of Asia is to be found here. So you can have Scottish pine trees growing next to palm trees from the Sahara, and in the Bible days all the wild animals were here – lions, bears, crocodiles, camels – you have got the whole world squeezed into this little point where they all join. Fascinating, once you have got a feel of the geography and especially a feel for the shape of the land.

The map of the Promised Land is a relief map. Can you see that deep valley running north-south and then the desert? If you master that map and hold it in your mind, you will be able to read every Bible story that takes place in the Promised Land very easily, and you will know why things happened as they did, and why Samaria was in the middle and why Jesus' main ministry was up in Galilee; why he was put to death by the Jews – that does not mean by all Israelis, it means the people of Judah. And when you read in the Gospel of John that the Jews killed Jesus, that doesn't mean all Israel it means the Southerners up in the hills. The Galileans were all for Jesus. It was the Jews, the Judeans, who were against him in the south. So that is the geographical background for the Bible. In the Old Testament we are moving around that Fertile Crescent from one end to the other. Sometimes the people of God are slaves in Egypt, other times they are taken away into Assyria or Babylon, but there they were, right in the middle of it all, at the crossroads of the world.

Now the other dimension that you need to master is the dimension of time and I have tried to reduce this dimension of time to a very simple pattern that is easily held in your mind.

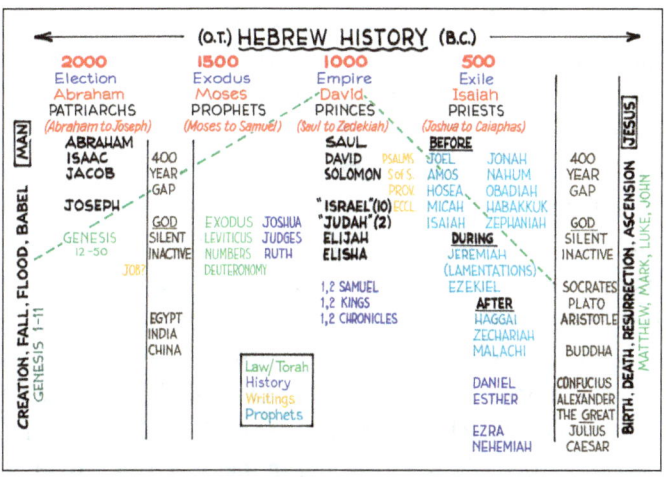

At first sight that chart must look horrific to you, but as we go through it I think you will find it is actually very simple. Basically, the Old Testament covers 2000 years of history – BC (Before Christ), but there is in Genesis 1 – 11, what we might call the pre-historic part; that means pre-historic to Israel and so in Genesis 1 – 11 we have the Creation of the universe, the Fall of man in the Garden of Eden, the flood and the tower of Babel. It is all about man generally. It is not about God's chosen people yet; it is about the human race, and that is the pre-historic history of Israel – before their history really began. But their history begins around the year 2000 BC, so just as far as we are after Christ, the history of Israel starts before Christ – two thousand years either side.

That is our opening date for the history of Israel and I divide it into four equal parts of 500 years each, and we take those four quarters as distinct periods. We mark each of the four dates (2000, 1500, 1000 and 500 BC) with events and people, and I like to give names of people and events to these dates so I fix them in my mind. So the first four words I have written down are events – Election, Exodus, Empire, Exile – and you have got the four events that mark the four quarters of their history. There is when God chose Abraham and elected Abraham and his descendants to be his people; there is when Moses led them out of Egypt; there is when they had all the land God promised to them and had a time of unparalleled prosperity and peace, and I have called it the Empire because they not only had their own land but many other nations were now under their control. And then there is the lowest point of their history: Exile. Roughly speaking, those four events fit those four dates. Then I attach a prominent person to each of those dates. Abraham is the man to attach to 2000, Moses to 1500 or thereabouts, David to 1000 (he was reigning in the year 1000 BC) and Isaiah is the most prominent man associated with the Exile. So, you have four events and four people. But also, the leadership of Israel changed, and the leadership in each of these four periods was different. In the first period they were led by Patriarchs (that is a word for forefathers really) from Abraham to Joseph. In the second period they were led by Prophets, from Moses to Samuel. In the third 500 years they were led by Princes, from Saul to Zedekiah, and in the fourth period they were led by Priests – from Joshua who came with Zerubbabel back from the Exile right through to Caiaphas in our Lord's day.

So you can see that the leadership changed from Patriarchs to Prophets to Princes and then to Priests. Now it doesn't mean there were not prophets at other times or priests at other times, but the leadership of the nation passed from one group to the other – until Jesus came, who was prophet, priest and king all rolled into one. So they tried three different kinds of leadership in their history but they were really looking for someone who could combine all these things in one, and all the leadership failed in the Old Testament.

So have you got those four basic periods in your mind? Now once you have got that, the next thing is to put in two gaps – each of them 400 years. During those 400 years, on both occasions, God said nothing and he did nothing so there is nothing in your Bible from those two periods. Now of course there are books written in those two periods but they are not in our Bible because they do not cover the time when God was saying and doing things. You see, when we read this phrase in the Bible 'the living God', do you realise what that means? Well did you realise a few years ago what it meant when some theologians started saying 'God is dead'? Have you heard that phrase? They did not mean that God has ceased to exist – that was a popular misunderstanding. What they meant was God is no longer active in this world; that he still exists but he is somewhere else now. As you may know my wife and I lost our daughter – she was 36. She is dead; that does not mean she has ceased to exist. She is alive, she is conscious, she is communicating, though she can't communicate with us now. But she is not living now – by that we mean she is not speaking and acting in this world as she was, but she's fully conscious and communicating elsewhere and she is with the Lord, you see. So she is alive but she is not living in this world; as far as this world goes, she is dead. Now that is what the 'living God' means and during these two periods God was 'dead', if you like. You see, he was not acting in this world, he was out of touch, and so the books written in these periods were the Apocrypha and you will not find them in our Bibles. The Catholics put them in their Bibles because they find prayers to the saints, and purgatory in the Apocrypha – that is why they put it in. But in fact it doesn't belong to the Bible because those books were written in a day when God was not living, but in *these* periods he was the living God – he was speaking and acting in our world.

Now you have got those two gaps – the gap that occurred in the first quarter, and the gap that occurred in the last quarter – and that is why Malachi is the last book in your Old Testament though there is a 400-year gap before Matthew comes along – because God was not saying anything, he was not doing anything so we are not interested in the history. It is just like any other history then, and similarly we have got nothing between Genesis and Exodus though there is a 400-year gap there, and we often miss that when we read straight on, but Exodus makes it clear there is a 400-year gap. It is interesting what happened during gaps when God was silent and inactive. The Egyptian, the Indian and the Chinese cultures developed in one gap, and in a gap, you had people like Socrates, Plato and Aristotle and the Greek philosophy that has influenced the Western world so much; you had Buddha, Confucius and then you had people like Alexander the Great and Julius Caesar. You see, when God is not busy, man is. So much has happened in man's history that is really not of relevance to God because it is what God's history contains that is of importance to us.

Now let us look at some details. Genesis 12–50 picks up the first period of Israel's history when they were led by patriarchs, and it is possible that the book of Job comes in there as well. Everything in Job is very much the sort of life that Abraham, Isaac and Jacob lived – the life of the travelling people of those days. Then we come to the next quarter and again we only have a few books from that quarter – Exodus, Leviticus, Numbers, Deuteronomy, all from Moses' lifetime; and then Joshua, Judges and Ruth continuing the history of that period. Then we have the empire days and we have more books: we have the record of the third quarter of their history in Samuel, Kings and Chronicles; but we also have some poetic books. We have David and the book of Psalms; Solomon and the Song of Solomon, Proverbs and Ecclesiastes. But after Solomon there was civil war and the twelve tribes divided into two: ten in the north who called themselves Israel; two in the south calling themselves Judah, and from then on, they did not have a united nation. There were prophets during that time, Elijah and Elisha, but they didn't write down for subsequent generations what they prophesied, so we don't have books called by their names. Then suddenly, we have a flood of books – all prophets and all associated with the Exile – and that is when the main books of prophecy are written, and some of them prophesied before the exile, some of them during the exile, and some after the exile, which tells us how important this event was in their history – the loss of the land God had promised them. Some prophets warned them they were going to lose the land. Some prophets comforted them when they did lose the land, and others were concerned with rebuilding the land when they came back after seventy years away. We have one or two history books from this period – Daniel and Esther were both about the Jews away from the land when they were in Babylon. Ezra and Nehemiah were the two men who helped to rebuild Jerusalem and get the people established back in their own land again.

Does that give you a feel of the Old Testament? Unfortunately, you see, the books of the Old Testament are not always in chronological order, especially the prophets. The history books seem to be, but when you get to the prophets they simply put the big ones first and the little ones second, which is terribly confusing. What I am saying is that of each of the prophet books you need to ask: was this written before the exile, during the exile, or after the exile? That will give you a clue to the understanding. Now I hope all is crystal clear, but if you can memorise the basic features of that with its two thousand years of history divided into five hundred years each, then you will get a really good grasp and then you fit the books in.

Of course, there are different types of books – there is the Law, the first five books, and you see where they fit in: Genesis before the gap and the other four after the gap. Then there are history books, and you see where they fit in. Then there are the writings, mainly poetry books, and you see that they come out of the period when they were most prosperous. That is when culture and art prosper. You see when the nation is rich and at peace that is when things like poetry get written. It is a luxury, is art (and culture), and you see it flourishing at the peak.

Now there is one more thing on the chart which I am sure you have noticed and that is a dotted line. You see, the peak of their fortunes was the empire under David; everything leads up to that and then everything goes downhill from then on, until they lose the land. It is a tragic story really, but that is why every Jew looks back to that period and longs for it to come back. That was the golden age – Lord, send us another David, send us a Messiah like David, send us the son of David – and still to this day the Jewish people are looking for that son of David to come back and restore the prosperity. The last question the disciples asked Jesus before he ascended to heaven was: when are you going to restore the kingdom to Israel? And still they are asking two thousand years later.

So that is the peak and their fortunes on the whole were up and up and up to that point, but from then down and down: civil war, division between the ten tribes of the north and the two in the south. It is all in the book of Kings which is a very sad and sordid tale when you read it through and of all the kings they had most of them were bad, many were assassinated. They had one dreadful queen – just one, because it was God's will they should only have kings, and they had the one dreadful queen.

After this 400-year gap during which they had no words from God and did not see a single miracle, suddenly it all started again and John the Baptist came preaching – the first prophet for a long time. Then the miracles came with Jesus, and the birth, death, resurrection and ascension of Jesus starts our New Testament, which only covers a hundred years or less. So your whole New Testament was written in one hundred years whereas the Old Testament was written over two thousand, and if you go back to Creation, how long...?

That is the chart that I hold in my mind and, by the way, a friend of mine called Professor LaGard Smith who is the Professor of Law in the Pepperdine University in Malibu (and my wife was Pepperdine before I changed her name) has produced a unique Bible with no chapter and verse numbers and that Bible is in chronological order so that you get to the prophets at the right time and you read the story in the order in which God spoke and acted, and it is quite a book. The only divisions in it are where there is a star in the margin every so often and altogether there are 365 stars in the margin. Can you guess why? It means you can read the whole story of God in a year. It is about five pages each day and you will get the Word of God in its proper context of time and place with some very helpful little notes of introduction. It really is a fascinating production and it is now available. I don't have a commission on selling it, but there it is; he is a friend.

Well now, that has perhaps put us into the history side, and we have looked at the geography side, but let us now look at one other complication and that is there is a big difference between our English Bible and the Hebrew Bible. I am afraid those who arranged our English Bible did not do us a very great service because we have therefore tended to think of books rather differently from the way the Jew thinks of the scriptures in the Old Testament. We tend in English to divide the books between three categories and I partly did that on the previous chart. We tend to think of the history books – and all the history books are put together in English from Genesis through to Esther, and they are all at the beginning of our Old Testament and they are in chronological order and that is helpful to get the history line – but it is not helpful from another point of view.

The next group of books in our Bibles are poetry: the book of Job which is all poetry; Psalms, Proverbs – poetry; Ecclesiastes and Song of Solomon. So the poetry books have been pushed together as the second grouping. Now even though they are in groups, it is very rare for an English Bible to have a heading 'History' or 'Poetry', so the books just run on one after another and we tend not to realise we have moved into a different group of books. And then all the prophetic books are listed, and they are divided between the major and the minor. I am sure you have heard those words: major prophets; minor prophets. All it means is some are big ones and some are little ones – not people or in message, but just how much they spoke or how much we have of their message. We have a lot of Isaiah, a lot of Jeremiah, a lot of Ezekiel, but very little of Joel or Obadiah, so the big books are called major and the twelve smaller books minor, and that is how the English Old Testament is arranged and frankly it is not very helpful. Pity, but there it is.

When you read the Hebrew scriptures, they have three very clear divisions – very different from one another. The first five books are not regarded as history at all but as

Law, and I have already explained that, and therefore they are not called Genesis, Exodus, Leviticus, Numbers and Deuteronomy; they are given the titles of the first words on the scroll as you unroll it so that you recognise it straight away to read it. And these books were read, and still are every year in the synagogue, right through on a lectionary. Then the big surprise comes that the next group are called the 'prophets', and they put into the prophets what we call history – Joshua, Judges, Samuel and Kings – but they call them the former prophets. Then they call others latter prophets. Now why should they call those books 'prophets'? Well, of course, there are prophets in them. Joshua was a prophet, Samuel was a prophet – that is not the reason why. The reason is that this is prophetic history, and prophetic history is quite different from other history and I need to explain why.

All history is based on two principles. Selection is the first, and connection is the second, and when anybody writes a history book, the first thing they must do is select what they are going to put in and what they are going to leave out. Nobody can write a complete history about anybody or anything. In fact, John's Gospel says if everything Jesus did and said was written down, the world could not hold the books. So every bit of history is a selection of some events and every historian selects what he thinks is important. And the second principle is the principle of connection – having selected the important events the historian then tries to show the connection between those events – that this led to that, and that led to the other. Do you follow me? And all history books are based on those two principles: what to select, and how to connect. Now prophetic history has its own answer to those two principles. Prophetic history only selects what is important to God – that is why there's nothing about Buddha or Confucius in the Bible. It only selects what is important to God and then it connects up what happens to people with God, and that is the connection.

Therefore, these books are written from a prophetic point of view – they only select what is important to God and they connect everything with God. That is why they are called by the Jews 'former prophets'. You notice the book of Ruth is not there and the books of Chronicles are not there because neither Ruth nor Chronicles are prophetic history. Certainly, the story of Ruth came where the English Bible puts it, between Judges and Samuel. That is where it happened, but if you read the story of Ruth, God says nothing in it and he does nothing in it, have you noticed? It is a lovely story, and it is the story of David's ancestor, but there is not a single 'Thus saith the Lord' in the book of Ruth; and Chronicles also; though it sounds like Kings, when you study it carefully it is quite different from the Kings and it is not a prophetic book, it is written from an entirely different point of view.

So they have the former and the latter prophets and then they put everything else in the writings. That is where they put Chronicles though they call it 'the words of the days'; that is where they put Ruth and they also put the poetry books. They put Ecclesiastes there, though they call it 'The Preacher', and Lamentations is just called 'How'! That is the first word of the book actually, and Esther is there, even Daniel. Daniel is not among the prophets. There is a reason for all that.

It is interesting that on the road to Emmaus and during his resurrection Jesus did Bible studies. He never did that during his life, but after he rose from the dead he gave Bible studies for the first time, and it says he took them through the Law, the prophets and the writings, and showed them everything concerning himself. So for Jesus that was the Old Testament and I personally believe it should be that for us as well, because it helps us to realise that it is not straight history. It

is prophetic history and it has, therefore, a message for us.

The books of the Apocrypha are history books and for example there is a fascinating little bit of Hebrew or Israeli history in the days of the Maccabees when they rebelled against the Greeks who were occupying the land, and it has been made into oratorios. "Maccabees" is very moving history but it is only history; you can read it if you are interested, but it will not speak to you from God because it is not prophetic, and prophetic history speaks to us today. That is why God is able to speak to you through the books of the Old Testament. But if I were teaching you the book of the Maccabees that would not happen. It would be interesting, but that is all. So can you see the importance of seeing this not as history at all, but as seeing it as God's law and God's prophecy, and seeing these others as kind of miscellaneous? Then what was the principle behind the selection? Why didn't they put the Apocrypha in there? The answer is that all these Bible books were written during the period when God was living – meaning by that: when God was active in this world. So all these books came out of that same prophetic period, that same time when God was busy. None of these books were written in the gaps. So we have got in our Bible the Law of God, the prophetic history, and also all the other books that came out of the period when God was busy with his people.

Can you see the shape of the Old Testament? Now we can see how it all fits in. Let me mention a chart that I used when I looked at Genesis. The first five books of the Bible are very special; they are basic to the whole Bible. They are the Law of Moses, the five books of Moses, the Torah. There is a very interesting pattern. Do you remember a string-shaped game and shape called a diabolo? Keep that shape in your mind when you look at the first five books of the Bible: Genesis, which means beginnings; Exodus, which means going out; Leviticus, as it says, is about the Levites; Numbers is self-explanatory. 'Deutero' means second and 'nomos' means law – second law. The Ten Commandments were given, and a second time; but look at this amazing pattern. Genesis is concerned with the whole human race; Exodus is the beginning of their national life, Leviticus is concerned with one tribe, the Levites; Numbers is concerned with national life, and Deuteronomy looks again to the history of the whole world. Then look at the *places*. It starts in Chaldea, then Canaan, then Egypt, then at Sinai, then through the Negev and Edam, Moab, and back into the Promised Land. Look at *when* – Genesis covers centuries, Exodus only covers years (300); Leviticus covers only one month. Numbers covers years again, and Deuteronomy covers centuries again. It is an amazing pattern when you see it all put beautifully together, but those five books are in a sense the most important part of the Old Testament, and the more you know about them the more you will understand the rest of the Old Testament and indeed the New. So the Jews are right to put a special emphasis on these five books. They are the foundation of the Bible.

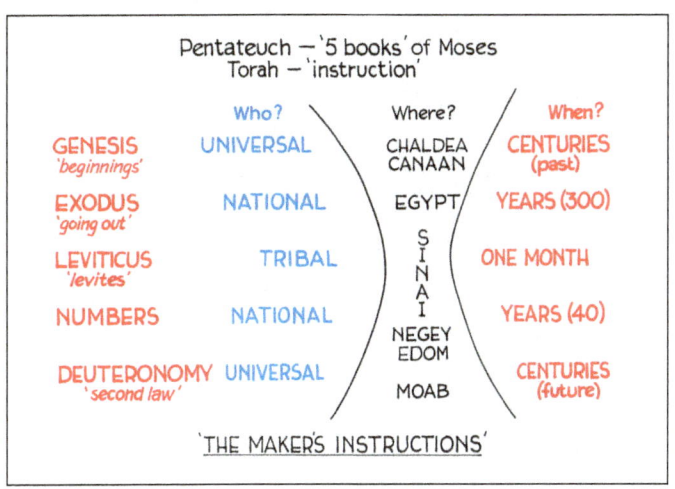

HEBREW POETRY

Let us turn to Hebrew poetry. Fortunately, most of our modern Bibles print poetry as poetry and prose as prose, and it is very important that they do. For example, prose is printed like a newspaper column with no gaps between the sentences, and every bit of space is filled, and the unit is the paragraph. So that is prose, but poetry has lots more space in it, much shorter lines, and it is set out in verses, and the basic unit is the verse and not the paragraph. Now why should that be important – prose and poetry? And why is it important to have a Bible that shows you the difference? Because English poetry is a little different from Hebrew poetry, so it does not always appear as clear to us as it should. When God speaks in prose, he is communicating thoughts from his mind to your mind, but when he speaks in poetry he is communicating his feelings from his heart to your heart. So that should be a real key to unlock the Bible for you. When you read poetry in the Bible, you should be asking about the *feelings* of God and there is a tremendous lot in the Bible about God's emotions. God feels, and we affect his feelings every day. This day we may make him sad or happy or angry, so that we are affecting God's feelings constantly and in fact, what we feel about God is not nearly so important as what he feels about us. So it is important to study poetry and prose, and I am going to look at poetry now.

Most of the prophets wrote in and spoke in poetry, which means that they were really speaking from the heart of God about how God was feeling, and that is very important. You see you can be too intellectual in your study of the Bible; you can just get nice thoughts from it, but you need to feel God's feelings as well as think his thoughts, and the Bible communicates his feelings in poetry. Now prose is a more normal, natural form of speech. When we talk to each other we use prose. It would be rather odd if we used poetry; it is in a sense artificial – it has to be composed. You have to think about what you are going to say before you say it with poetry, whereas prose you can just get straight into. For example, supposing I came home and said to Enid:

> I'm ready for my supper wife,
> Oh, good it's pies and peas;
> You've given me a dirty knife;
> I'd like a clean one please!
> And since there is no second course,
> I'll have some more tomato sauce!

Now that is not the way I talk when I come in. If I talked like that it means I have done a lot of thinking about it before I come in; it is an artificial form of speech. It is not normal speech it is special speech. Then why use it? Why bother to compose poetry? Well the answer is it has a much deeper appeal to people and therefore is likely to have a greater influence on them. It reaches the parts that prose cannot reach. That is why you find poetry in greeting cards, Valentine cards, birthday cards and Christmas cards, because they are a heart message and so we say it in poetry rather than prose. Beginning to get a feel? That is a good phrase to use actually – to get a *feel* for poetry.

First of all, poetry goes deeper into the mind; it stays in the memory much longer. It is much easier to remember poems from your school days than the prose that you were taught, isn't it? You can recite poetry you learned as a child; it stays in the mind. Most of us learn our theology from hymns and songs. Why? Because it is poetry – and that is why it is so important that you have songs with content. Some of the songs today have little content, but if you really soak yourself in the didactic hymns of Charles Wesley, you are really going to have a lot of knowledge. They are much easier to remember, so they go deeper into the mind, into the intuitive and artistic hemisphere of your brain which holds on to things better. The second thing is that they go deeper into the heart, they touch your feelings. Let me touch your feelings with a little poem.

> They walked down the lane together,
> The sky was full of stars,
> Together they reached the farmyard gate,
> He lifted for her the bars.
> She neither smiled nor thanked him,
> Indeed she knew not how,
> For he was just a farmer's boy,
> And she was a Jersey cow!

Now, that poem touched two feelings in you. It touched your romantic feelings and your heart maybe began to beat a bit quicker, wondering what was coming, and then when it came it touched your sense of humour and your fun. You see now if I had said that in prose, it would not have had nearly the same effect. And then poetry goes deeper into the will. It can challenge you at a deeper level than prose – to change your way of life. One of the poems that I have quoted many times when I have preached was written by the famous army chaplain of the First World War, Studdert Kennedy, who became known as Woodbine Willy because he gave out cheap Woodbine cigarettes to the soldiers, and then became a vicar in Shrewsbury in a church that is now a Pentecostal Assembly. I have preached in it and thought of him. His wonderful poem is called 'Indifference'. Now listen to this poem for bringing a challenge to your will.

When Jesus came to Golgotha they hanged him on a tree,
They drove great nails through hands and feet
And made a Calvary.
They crowned him with a crown of thorns,
Red were his wounds and deep,
For those were crude and cruel days,
And human flesh was cheap.

When Jesus came to Birmingham,
They simply passed him by,
They never hurt a hair of him,
They only let him die.
For men had grown more tender,
And they would not give him pain,
They only passed him down the street,
And left him in the rain.

Still Jesus cried 'forgive them, for they know
Not what they do',
And still it rained the wintery rain that drenched him
Through and through.
The crowds went home and left the streets,
Without a soul to see,
But Jesus crouched against a wall,
And cried for Calvary.

See how that poem really gets you? So that is why the Hebrews used poetry – it can touch the whole person, heart, mind, and will, and therefore God has used it a great deal.

Now the key to poetry is to make words beautiful as well as meaningful. That is what draws us to poetry; the words are arranged in such a way that they appeal to our sense of beauty which is basically a sense of balance, of symmetry, of proportion. A beautiful person has well balanced features and it is this symmetry, this balance, that appeals to us in poetry. There is a beautiful balance about the words – the lines are the same length. Now there are three types or three basic features of poetry which make the word beautiful for us. First of all, there is rhyme. That is a big feature of English poetry but not of Hebrew poetry. But rhyme is very popular with us – the balance of rhyming words.

> Jack and Jill went up the hill, to fetch a pail of water,
> Jack fell down and broke his crown
> and Jill came tumbling after.

There is rhyming all the way through, and most nursery rhymes are built on rhyme for their appeal. John Betjeman was mainly building on rhyme in his poems. Now we have blank verse and never know whether it is poetry or not, but if the words are arranged beautifully it is, but it certainly does not depend on rhyme. Nowadays the shock line has value:

> Thirty days hath September,
> April, June and November;
> All the rest have 31.
> Is that fair?!

A line comes in which startles you and breaks the rhythm and brings you up with a jerk, and therefore all poetry depends on the irregularity as well as the regularity.

The second major feature is rhythm; the beat also makes

speech beautiful. We call it the metre, based on syllables; the limerick is a classic case and it always follows the same rhythm.

Now this is true of Hebrew poetry. A favourite rhythm in English poetry is what we call the 4/3 rhythm – *The boy stood on the burning deck whence all but he had fled.* That is 4/3 beat and that is very common in Hebrew poetry too. It is common in the metrical Psalms in Scotland – *The Lord's my shepherd I'll not want* – 4; *He makes me down to lie* – 3; *in pastures green he leadeth me* – 4; *the quiet waters by* – 3. 4, 3, 4, 3. Somehow that sticks in our mind, it is a rhythm that fixes the words for us. So that is the second thing.

Now with rhythm it is terribly important that the emphasis falls on the right syllable. Again, I have to say in a lot of choruses today the beat is on the wrong syllable every time. If I give you just one – *For all the good our Father does, God and king of us all.* Now, doesn't that jar? Because the beat comes on the 'and' instead of 'God'. And that is one of the differences between good and bad choruses and good and bad poetry. If the beat is not on the right word it doesn't reach us, and you find in Hebrew poetry the rhythm is on the right word, but of course that is in Hebrew – not so easy to translate it into English.

The other thing that enhances poetry is repetition, so we have rhyming, rhythm and repetition, and the repetition of a word or a line makes it poetic. *And Brutus is an honourable man, and Brutus is an honourable man* – somehow the repetition becomes poetic to us. Or *Baa, baa, black sheep have you any wool? Yes sir, yes sir* – repetition of a word and it becomes a balance. We have got two eyes, two ears, two nostrils, two arms, two legs, and so a double repetition of a word becomes poetic; it becomes balanced and symmetrical to us. So especially twice repetition.

Pleasant sounds are a key and poetry is meant to be read

aloud. You don't really get poetry if you just read it with your eyes – which means that if you are going to use the Psalms, for example, read them aloud. You are far more likely to get something from reading the poetry of the Bible aloud than just reading it silently. There is something very satisfying about the sound of poetry; it depends on sound, the content is nicely packaged, and poetry brings *wonder* into things. There is a sense of wonder in poetry that there is not in prose, and wonder is half way to worship. That is why the Psalms are all in poetry.

I have some versions here of a nursery rhyme –

*Twinkle, twinkle little star, how I wonder what you are,
up above the world so high, like a diamond in the sky.*

You can kill the childlike wonder in that poem by reducing it to scientific terms. Here is another version I came across –

*Twinkle, twinkle little star, I don't wonder what you are,
you're the cooling down of gases, forming into solid masses!*

Now do you notice the childlike wonder has gone? Let us take it a step further –

*Scintillate, scintillate, globule prolific,
fair would I fathom thy nature specific,
loftily poised in ether capacious,
closely resembling a gem carbonaceous.*

It is the same poem, but it is killed dead; it has gone scientific and in a sense, prose is scientific language of the mind, but poetry is wonder language of the heart. There is a childlike quality about it.

Well, all that is about poetry generally. And one other feature of poetry is that it is visual as well as verbal. It constantly paints pictures in the mind that you can *see*. Images – imagination is very necessary to writing poetry and it uses lots of metaphors, lots of similes, lots of images - like twinkle, twinkle little star, like a diamond in the sky – that is a picture; you can see the diamond. Or in the Psalms, *As the deer pants for streams of water, so my soul longs for God*. There is a picture there of an animal with its tongue hanging out panting – as a deer pants, so my soul longs for God.

So far we have been considering English poetry which is based on Greek and Roman, where the emphasis is on the sound, but in Hebrew poetry that is not the case, the emphasis is on the sense. That is because if you are not careful, the sound can override the sense and you can appreciate the sound of poetry and get no message from it. That of course is why the English are known for nonsense verse – Edward Lear and Lewis Carol were masters of it. Do you know the Jabberwocky? Listen to the beat of this –

> *Twas brillig, and the slithy toves*
> *Did gyre and gimble in the wabe,*
> *All mimsy were the borogoves,*
> *And the mome raths outgrabe.*

Do you get it? Beautiful poetry, It is wonderful poetry to read, fascinating – but the message? What message? You see, it is wasted. Now that is why Hebrew poetry put the emphasis not on the sound of the words but on the *sense* of the words and therefore, we look always for the sense. That is why there is very little rhyme in Hebrew poetry. There is some rhythm, especially the 4/3 and the 3/3, but mostly it is based on repetition, and that is the key to Hebrew poetry; it is in fact repetition. We therefore call it parallelism and it is based on the two-fold repetition. I have said we have two eyes, two arms, two legs; two of a thing give it balance and therefore most Hebrew poetry is in what we call couplet form – two statements that belong together and these two statements are related in different ways to give us a bit of variety. Sometimes the second statement is the same all the way through the psalm. A statement is made and then *for his mercy endures for ever,* another statement – *for his mercy endures for ever.* So that is one very simple form of Hebrew poetry: to have a refrain as the second half of each couplet. It really is effective because a couplet enables you to have what we call antiphonal singing, which means two choirs singing against each other, or *to* each other, and so one choir sings the first sentence and the other choir echoes it with the other sentence and there is that echo. The Psalms are very meaningful if you read or sing them antiphonally like that – and one half sings, or reads, or says the first line and the other the second. Try it some time.

You see, in the New Testament they use psalms in worship and we should. Again, unfortunately, modern choruses usually contain no more than one or two verses of a psalm and therefore, miss the context and it is so important to take the psalm as a whole, so encourage your church to use psalms as a whole. If you cannot sing them, then say them, but read them like this, as a couplet – one voice and then another. Now the three ways in which they are related to each other, this parallelism, is an echo. Take a typical verse:

Where can I go from your spirit?
Where can I flee from your presence?

That is Hebrew poetry – it is the same thing said twice. The second line echoes the first and gives a beautiful balance and symmetry to what is being said. Having said it twice, of course, it sticks in your mind and the thought is there twice. When I am preaching in another language I have to do it through what we call an 'interrupter' who steals half my time, but those who know English of course get the message twice and they really get so much from it because they hear each sentence first in English from me and then in the language from the interpreter. They get far more than the others who know only one language. So this repetition is very good for emphasis – saying a thing twice; it is very good for response; this echo is very good for balance, but it is not just simple repetition. The second line usually takes the thought of the first line a step further. It does that in a number of ways. Let us take an example from Psalm six: *O Lord, do not rebuke me in your anger or discipline me in your wrath*. You see, rebuking is just being told, but discipline is being punished. So the second line has taken the same thought a little further. Don't rebuke me and then don't discipline me – and yet they belong together; they are poetic.

Or take the next verse.

Be merciful to me O Lord, for I am faint;
O Lord, heal me for my bones are in agony.

Now in the first line he is just feeling faint but in the second line he is in agony and needing healing. So once again the second line has taken the first line a little further. Now I hope all this is not destroying poetry for you, because really analysing poetry is like taking a flower to pieces and pulling the petals off and looking at the stamen and so on, and it destroys it. Poetry needs to be experienced in its beauty, but I want to help you to understand what is going on when you read a psalm, why it was written and how it was written.

Now there are three major types of couplet – what we call synonymous, in which the same thought is said in different words (that is what we have been talking about so far); then there is antithetic in which the second line as it were, contradicts or rather presents a contrast to the first line, and the balance is by way of contrast. So for example: *Those who sow in tears will reap with songs of joy.* Now, do you see the contrast? Sowing and reaping; tears, joy. So now the couplet has a contrast built in — that is what we call antithetic couplets. It is the opposite thought. So synonymous is the same thought but in different words - it may be just simply repeated like the first I gave you, or it may take it further as we looked at. But both of those are really the same thought expressed differently. But now we have opposite thought expressed together – *He who goes out reaping, carrying seed to sow, will return with songs of joy carrying sheaves with him.* Now that has taken these two lines much further – for now we have reaping and sheaves, and we have sowing and seed, and going out and returning.

Then we have what we call synthetic couplets, and synthetic couplets *add* to the first thought, they don't repeat it and they don't contrast it, but they add much more to it. *The Lord is my shepherd I shall not want.* Now the second is the result of the first; the first is the cause, the second is the effect; and the 23rd Psalm is built on that pattern we call the synthetic. *He makes me lie down in green pastures* – that thought is not repeated, but – *He leads me beside still waters* and how meaningful those last two lines become when you study shepherding in the Middle East. You see, there is not green grass everywhere and you cannot just put sheep into a field and let them graze. You have to go up to fifteen miles a day to find some green grass growing, and a good shepherd knows where the green pastures are. But furthermore, a sheep's nostrils are next door to its mouth, much closer to their mouth than our nose is to mouth. The result is they cannot drink unless the water is still. If they try to drink in troubled or running water, they will drown. They will sniff water up into their nostrils. So the shepherd has to know where there is green pasture and where there is still water. But those two things together create a picture of a shepherd who really knows his job and is able to do this for the sheep. Now that is synthetic poetry.

So we have these three forms of poetry, but many varieties within these forms, and you will find that these patterns are constantly broken by irregularities just to keep the interest and to make it sparkle a bit. So sometimes the rhythm is broken and sometimes the pattern is broken. Sometimes instead of two lines there are three lines together. Let's just look at some of them. For example, here are three lines from Psalm 29 –

Ascribe to the Lord oh mighty ones!
Ascribe to the Lord glory and strength,
Ascribe to the Lord the glory due to his name.

Now there is a three – a tricolon we call it – and so it has built up a crescendo. *Ascribe to the Lord!* is the refrain, and then different words are added in three lines.

Or here is another - from Psalm 3 –

O Lord! How many are my foes,
How many rise up against me?
How many are saying of me God will not deliver him.

Now you have the repetition: "how many, how many, how many", but the wording is different, and each sentence builds on the previous one. Then sometimes there is an omission and a word is not included or a phrase drops out. Full of pictures – "as the hart pants"; I have told you that one.
As a father pities his children so the Lord pities those who fear him. There is a picture of a tender father with his children. Then sometimes the lines cross over and the first

part of the first line becomes the second part of the second line. Let us take an example:

> *For the Lord watches over the way of the righteous*
> *but the way of the wicked will perish....*

There "the way" has swapped places.

All this is just to help you to appreciate the Hebrew poetry much more. There is sometimes a kind of staircase in it, which it kind of climbs up. For example, here is a little staircase verse:

> *The voice of Yahweh breaks the cedars,*
> *Yahweh breaks the cedars of Lebanon....*

So there is an introduction of something new in that second line, namely cedars of Lebanon. Sometimes the poetry is based on the alphabet. I recall an old pop song from many years ago – "A, you're adorable, B, you're so beautiful, C you're a cutie...." That is an acrostic poem and it is based on the alphabet and many psalms are based on the alphabet. The first verse is *aleph* (A in Hebrew) and in Psalm 119, a very long one, it goes on and on and on and there every verse in a section begins with a new letter of the alphabet, all the way through. It is artificial and some people say "Well, I think we should be natural when we speak to God; I don't think we should be artificial; we should be spontaneous, we should just say what comes into our heads." If you do that, you will only use prose to address God. But I think we should use poetry as well because that makes you think what you want to say. You have to prepare what you want to say and that is how most choruses and hymns get written. Somebody sits down and says: what do I want to say to God? They think about it and they prepare, and we use artificial speech whenever we sing a hymn, but it enables us to sing it together. If I just said to a congregation "Now the next time we worship, each of you sing whatever you really want to say to God", we are going to have chaos. It then becomes individual worship not corporate worship, and so the advantage of using poetry in worship is that we can say it together.

There used to be a family tradition in our house: our three children used to come and wake me up at an ungodly hour on a certain day in the year, and then they stood in a row at the foot of my bed, three of them, and then in a most artificial way they addressed me in poetry and after they had done that they then gave me a bag of their favourite sweets! They stood there and sang "Happy birthday to you". Now in a sense that was artificial, the three of them standing in a row and all saying the same thing. Wouldn't it have been nicer if each of them had come separately and told me what they really felt, and said, "Daddy, I love you"? No, because they would then not be my family. Do you understand what I am saying? The fact that they would come together and sing together meant more to *me*, because of their relationship with each other. It pleases the Lord when we say something together but of course we have to use artificial speech, we have to use words that somebody else has written, but God loves to see us together – standing in a row and singing to God, but we are nevertheless expressing "God, we're coming together to do this." And poetry enables us to do that. So I am glad it is in poetry.

Hebrew poetry is easy to use in other languages. Poems that depend on rhyme are very difficult to take into another language because the words in another language will not rhyme. I have tried, and I like quoting a poem when I preach. When I have an interpreter, it kills it dead, and it just does not come across. The big advantage of Hebrew poetry is that it can be so translated, and even in English the poetry comes across – the balance of the couplets comes across.

Do you think poetry touches God's heart as well as ours? I believe it does, and I believe King David knew that, and the prophets knew that they could reach human hearts better with poetry than prose. And I think that is why they used it, which means they must really have thought about what they wanted to say and thought in God's presence and let the Holy Spirit put what they wanted to say into poetry, so they could say it in a way that people could not forget. I believe it touches God's heart and that he likes poetry. There are so many things in God that appear in us. You know that God walks, so walking is the healthiest exercise we can take. You know that God sings. Zephaniah is the prophet who tells us that God bursts into song over *us*, and *rejoices over us* with singing. And that is why we sing. You know that God whistles, don't you? Go and read the first few chapters of Isaiah if you don't believe me. You say what translation is that? Any translation. God whistles, so we can whistle.

But I believe poetry touches his heart because it means that somebody has given a bit of thought to what they want to say, somebody has really given a bit of time: how can I best address this to God? And somebody has produced a chorus or a hymn that is beautiful.

HEBREW POETRY

"PARALLELISM" Thought-rhyme
Balance of SENSE, not SOUND

1. SYNONYMOUS   Same thought - different words

a. SIMPLY REPEATED
"Where can I go from your spirit?"
"Where can I flee from your presence?"

b. TAKEN FURTHER
"O Lord, do not rebuke me in your anger,
Or discipline me in your wrath
Be merciful to me, O Lord, for I am faint,
O Lord, heal me, for my bones are in agony."

2. ANTITHETIC   Opposite thought
"Those who sow in tears
Will reap with songs of joy.
He who goes out reaping, carrying seed to sow,
Will return with songs of joy, carrying sheaves with him."

3. SYNTHETIC   Added thought
"The Lord is my shepherd,
I shall not want;
He makes me lie down in green pastures
He leads me beside still waters."

ABOUT DAVID PAWSON

A speaker and author with uncompromising faithfulness to the Holy Scriptures, David brings clarity and a message of urgency to Christians to uncover hidden treasures in God's Word.

Born in England in 1930, David began his career with a degree in Agriculture from Durham University. When God intervened and called him to become a Minister, he completed an MA in Theology at Cambridge University and served as a Chaplain in the Royal Air Force for three years. He moved on to pastor several churches, including the Millmead Centre in Guildford, which became a model for many UK church leaders. In 1979, the Lord led him into an international ministry. His current itinerant ministry is predominantly to church leaders. David and his wife Enid currently reside in the county of Hampshire in the UK.

Over the years, he has written a large number of books, booklets, and daily reading notes. His extensive and very accessible overviews of the books of the Bible have been published and recorded in *Unlocking the Bible*. Millions of copies of his teachings have been distributed in more than 120 countries, providing a solid biblical foundation.

He is reputed to be the "most influential Western preacher in China" through the broadcast of his best-selling *Unlocking the Bible* series into every Chinese province by Good TV. In the UK, David's teachings are often broadcast on Revelation TV.

Countless believers worldwide have also benefited from his generous decision in 2011 to make available his extensive audio video teaching library free of charge at **www.davidpawson.org** and we have recently uploaded all of David's video to a dedicated channel on **www.youtube.com**

TAKE A LOOK AT YOUTUBE
www.youtube.com/user/DavidPawsonMinistry

THE EXPLAINING SERIES
BIBLICAL TRUTH SIMPLY EXPLAINED

If you have been blessed reading this book, we have more books available in David's Explaining Series. Please register to download for free by visiting
www.explainingbiblicaltruth.global

Other booklets in the *Explaining* series include:
The Amazing Story of Jesus
The Resurrection: *The Heart of Christianity*
Studying the Bible
Being Anointed and Filled with the Holy Spirit
New Testament Baptism
How to study a book of the Bible: Jude
The Key Steps to Becoming a Christian
What the Bible says about Money
What the Bible says about Work
Grace – *Undeserved Favour, Irresistible Force or Unconditional Forgiveness?*
Eternally secure? – *What the Bible says about being saved*
De-Greecing the Church – *The impact of Greek thinking on Christian beliefs*
Three texts often taken out of context: *Expounding the truth and exposing error*
The Trinity
The Truth about Christmas

They will also be available to purchase as print copies from:
Amazon or **www.thebookdepository.com**

OTHER TEACHINGS
BY DAVID PAWSON

For the most up to date list of David's Books
go to: **www.davidpawsonbooks.com**

To purchase David's teachings
go to: **www.davidpawson.com**

UNLOCKING THE BIBLE

A unique overview of both the Old and New Testaments, from internationally acclaimed evangelical speaker and author David Pawson. *Unlocking the Bible* opens up the Word of God in a fresh and powerful way. Avoiding the small detail of verse by verse studies, it sets out the epic story of God and his people in Israel. The culture, historical background and people are introduced and the teaching applied to the modern world. Eight volumes have been brought into one compact and easy to use guide to cover both the Old and New Testaments in one massive omnibus edition. *The Old Testament: The Maker's Instructions* (The five books of law); *A Land and A Kingdom* (Joshua, Judges, Ruth, 1&2 Samuel, 1&2 Kings); *Poems of Worship and Wisdom* (Psalms, Song of Solomon, Proverbs, Ecclesiastes, Job); *Decline and Fall of an Empire* (Isaiah, Jeremiah and other prophets); *The Struggle to Survive* (Chronicles and prophets of exile); *The New Testament: The Hinge of History* (Mathew, Mark, Luke, John and Acts); *The Thirteenth Apostle* (Paul and his letters); *Through Suffering to Glory* (Hebrews, the letters of James, Peter and Jude, the Book of Revelation). Already an international bestseller.

WATCH DAVID'S INTRO
www.davidpawson.com/utbintro

WATCH
www.davidpawson.com/utbwatch

LISTEN
www.davidpawson.com/utblisten

PURCHASE THE BOOK
www.davidpawson.com/utbbuybook

PURCHASE THE EBOOK
www.davidpawson.com/utbbuykindle

PURCHASE THE DVD
www.davidpawson.com/utbbuydvd

PURCHASE USB FLASH DRIVE INCLUDING:
- ALL VIDEO (MP4)
- ALL AUDIO TRACKS (MP3)
- CHARTS (PDF)

www.davidpawson.com/buyusb

OTHER LANGUAGES

Unlocking the Bible is available in book, video and audio formats and has been translated into other languages.

www.ingramcontent.com/pod-product-compliance
Lightning Source LLC
Chambersburg PA
CBHW071039080526
44587CB00015B/2683